MADONNA

Fellini

Peepshow
carnival
erotic
cabaret

androgynous

Edwardian

the Girlie Show

WORLD TOUR

70's platform
acid queen

girly show

THIS IS A
CALLAWAY
BoundSound™ Book

IN ASSOCIATION WITH **BOY TOY, INC.** AND

Winterland
productions

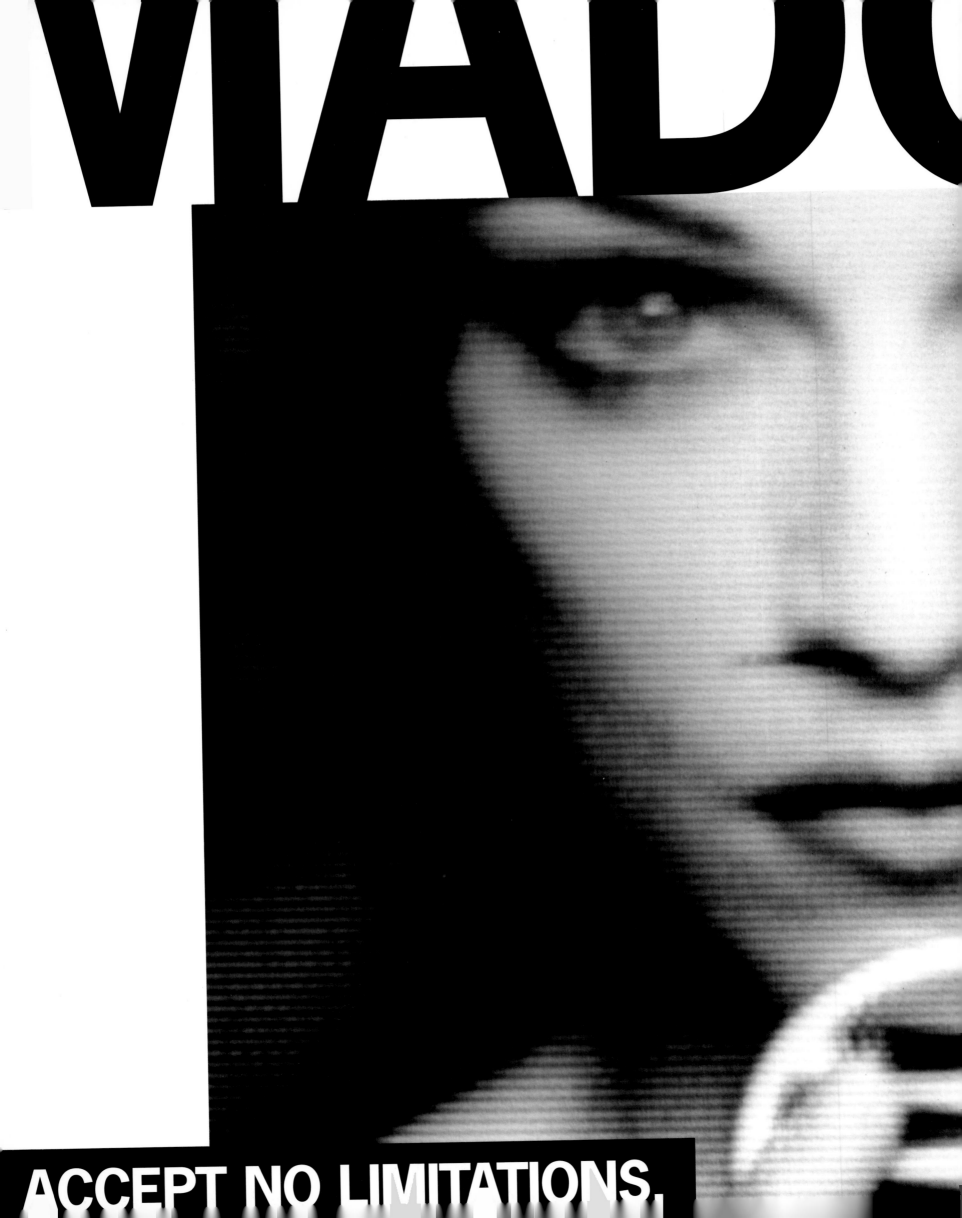

WHEN I FINISHED THE "BLONDE AMBITION" TOUR, I SWORE ON MY LIFE THAT I WOULD NEVER EVEN THINK OF GOING ON TOUR AGAIN AS LONG AS I LIVED. I WAS SPENT. I WAS EXHAUSTED. I WAS SICK OF TRAVELING. I WANTED STABILITY. SO, I THREW MYSELF INTO MAKING MOVIES, RECORDING A NEW ALBUM, AND I ALSO PUT OUT A BOOK CALLED SEX. SO MUCH FOR STABILITY.

NEEDLESS TO SAY, AS REWARDING AS ALL THESE CREATIVE ENDEAVORS WERE TO ME, THEY COULD NOT TAKE THE PLACE OF PERFORMING LIVE. THEATER IS MY LIFE—OR IS MY LIFE THEATER? I'M NOT SURE AND IT REALLY DOESN'T MATTER. BEING ON STAGE IS WHERE I FEEL MOST ALIVE, AND IT'S WHERE I'M ABLE TO PULL ALL OF MY CREATIVE ENERGIES INTO ONE OUTLET. IT'S THE ONLY PLACE WHERE I CAN COMBINE ALL OF MY INFLUENCES AND ALL OF MY INSPIRATIONS INTO ONE LIV- ING, BREATHING ANIMAL. THE STAGE IS THE ONLY ENVIRONMENT WHERE CUBIST PAINTING, BURLESQUE, FLAMENCO DANCING AND THE CIRCUS CAN LIVE TOGETHER UNDER ONE COZY ROOF. TAKING THE ADVENTURE ONE STEP FURTHER IS TO PLAY IN FRONT OF A DIFFERENT AUDIENCE EVERY NIGHT. DEALING WITH DIFFERENT CULTURES, DIFFERENT EXPECTATIONS, DIFFER- ENT WAYS OF EXPRESSING PLEASURE AND BEWILDERMENT— THIS TO ME IS THE ULTIMATE THRILL. THE ULTIMATE RISK. AND I LOVE TAKING RISKS. YOU MAY HAVE HEARD THAT ABOUT ME. THERE'S NO WAY THIS BOOK COULD TRULY RECAPTURE THE EXCITEMENT OF THE "GIRLIE SHOW," BUT IT COMES PRETTY DAMN CLOSE.

BY THE WAY, IF YOU EVER HEAR ME SAY, "I'M NEVER GOING ON TOUR AGAIN," DON'T BELIEVE ME.

ENJOY,

MADONNA

HURRY!
HURRY!

RIGHT THIS WAY.
STEP RIGHT UP, LADIES AND GENTLEMEN.
THE SHOW IS ABOUT TO BEGIN.
THIS IS THE GIRLIE SHOW.
THE ONE AND ONLY
OF ITS KIND.

SEE THE ONE AND ONLY MADONNA AND HER AMAZING TROUPE OF ECSYDISIASTS, HOOFERS AND TERPSICHOREANS, THESPIANS, MUMMERS, AND

FREAKS OF NATURE

PERFORMING A SPECTACLE UNLIKE ANY EVER SEEN ON THE FACE OF THE EARTH. NEVER BEFORE HAS A SHOW THIS ENTICING AND THIS PROVOCATIVE BEEN ENACTED HOOVE AND ON STAGE!   NEVER BEFORE HAS A STAR OF THIS MAGNITUDE TROUNCED SO MANY TABOOS AND BROACHED SO MANY BOUNDARIES, SEEMINGLY OBLIVIOUS TO THE SELF-APPOINTED ARBITRATORS OF DECENCY AND DECORUM.   LADIES AND GENTLEMEN, NEVER BEFORE HAS A CAST LIKE THIS BEEN ASSEMBLED.

IS IT MALE? IS IT FEMALE?

IS IT A COMBINATION OF THE TWO?

SEE THEIR GENDERS CHANGE BEFORE YOUR VERY EYES.

THEY SHIMMY. THEY SHAKE.

SEE THE INGENUES, THE SOUBRETTES AND SEDUCTRESSES! SEE AMAZING FEATS OF STRENGTH AND BALANCE THAT DEFY THE LAWS OF NATURE AND WILL CAUSE YOU TO QUESTION THE ACCURACY OF YOUR OWN SENSES. SEE THE SULTRY SYLPHS AND HOT-BLOODED HOURIS!

THEY CRAWL ON THEIR BELLIES LIKE REPTILES.

SEE STRANGE SCENES FROM FOREIGN CLIMES RE-ENACTED!

MADONNA HERSELF HANDPICKED THIS EXTRAORDINARY ASSEMBLY OF PULCHRITUDE AND BRAZEN VOLUPTUOUSNESS, SPENDING A YEAR PERSONALLY WANDERING THE DIVES, JOINTS, FLESHPOTS, DENS OF INIQUITY AND LOW RESORTS OF THE GLOBE, COLLECTING SUCH FASCINATING CREATURES THAT YOU WILL BE UNABLE TO AVERT YOUR EYES. NEVER BEFORE HAVE YOU SEEN SUCH STRANGE AND AFFECTING BEAUTIES, COMPORTING THEMSELVES IN A FRENZY OF EROTIC MESMERISM!

SEE THEM BUMP AND GRIND, PERFORMING THE MOST ANCIENT AND POWERFUL BODILY MOVEMENTS WITH UNPARALLELED EXPERTISE AND EFFECTIVENESS.

SEE THE CAN CAN, THE FAN DANCE AND THE FANDANGO!

THE NOTORIOUS MADONNA THE WORLD'S MOST FAMOUS STAR

WILL DEMONSTRATE TO ONE AND ALL

THE ENTIRE HISTORY OF THE GREATEST TRADITION IN SHOW BUSINESS—

THE GIRLIE SHOW.

BE WARNED, AT TIMES GENUINE PAGAN GODS MAY TAKE ACTUAL POSSESSION OF THE BODIES OF THE DANCERS, CAUSING CONTORTIONS AND GYRATIONS NEVER BEFORE SEEN IN THE CIVILIZED WORLD.

YOU'LL SEE MADONNA HERSELF, THE GREATEST STAGE PERFORMER IN THE HISTORY OF MAN'S ENTIRE EVOLUTION

CONTROLLING EVERY MUSCLE OF HER BODY WITH TOTAL PRECISION. SHE WILL WIGGLE, SHE WILL FLEX, SHE WILL GYRATE LIKE A TOP AND UNDULATE WITH THE FURY OF AN UNTAMED OCEAN. SHE HAS EVEN BEEN KNOW TO SING ON OCCASION. BUT BE WARNED, NO GLASSWARE WILL BE PERMITTED IN THE AUDITORIUM BECAUSE OF THE DEVASTATING POWER OF HER HIGHER REGISTERS.

LADIES AND GENTLEMEN, THE GIRLIE SHOW BRINGS A BRAND OF MAGIC TO THE STAGE, THE LIKES OF WHICH HAS NOT BEEN SEEN IN THIS CENTURY. YOU'LL SEE ILLUSION, DECEPTION, SLEIGHT OF HAND, LEGERDEMAIN AND TROMPE L'OEIL.

YOU'LL SEE BUFFOONS, JESTERS AND ZANIES. YOU'LL SEE MOTLEY FOOLS AND HARLEQUINS GATHERED FROM THE FOUR CORNERS OF THE EARTH FOR THEIR EXQUISITE RIDICULOUSNESS.

THEY'RE ALL HERE, FOLKS: PIERROT, SCARAMOUCHE, JACK PUDDING, PUNCH AND JUDY.

YOU'LL SEE COMEDY, YOU'LL SEE TRAGEDY, YOU'LL LAUGH 'TIL YOU CRY AND CRY 'TIL YOU LAUGH!

IS NOT
FOR
THE PRUDE,
THE
BLUENOSE
OR THE
FAINT
OF HEART.
IF
YOU ARE
SHOCKED BY
THE BEAUTY
OF THE
UNADORNED
BODY,
IF
YOU ARE
OFFENDED
BY GOD'S
MOST
INGENIOUS
AND
MASTERFUL
DESIGN,
THE HUMAN
FORM,
THIS SHOW
IS NOT FOR
YOU.

YOU MAY BLUSH, LADIES AND GENTLEMEN, BUT AS THE GREAT OSCAR WILDE ONCE REMARKED,

"THERE IS A GOOD DEAL TO BE SAID FOR BLUSHING, IF ONE CAN DO IT AT THE PROPER MOMENT."

IF
YOU ARE
A LIVING
AND BREATHING PERSON
WITH EVEN THE
NORMAL AMOUNT
OF EMOTION AND CURIOSITY,
YOU WILL BE THRILLED
AND TRANSPORTED
BEYOND YOUR
WILDEST EXPECTATIONS,
BY A SPECTACLE
WITHOUT PRECEDENT
IN THE HISTORY OF
GIRLYKIND

YOU MAY EVEN

LAUGH OR CRY

'TIL TEARS ROLL DOWN YOUR CHEEKS,

SO PLEASE, BRING YOUR HANDKERCHIEFS.

THE IMMORTAL CALL OF THE SIRENS WILL BE HEARD ONCE AGAIN.

■ MADONNA WILL CHANNEL CIRCE, LORELEI AND PARTHENOPE UNLEASHING AN UNPARALLELED ASSAULT OF ENTICEMENT, ALLUREMENT, TANTALIZATION AND ENCHANTMENT.

NO EXPENSE HAS BEEN SPARED ON THE COSTUMES AND SETS, WHICH ARE TRULY BIGGER THAN LIFE. THE WORLD'S LARGEST GO GO POLE ALONE IS WORTH THE PRICE OF ADMISSION.

IT'S ALL HERE FOLKS. THE INTRICATE CHOREOGRAPHY OF THE BROADWAY STAGE, THE HEARTPOUNDING POWER OF THE DISCOTHEQUE, THE BRAZEN SENSUALITY OF THE HOUSE OF BURLESQUE AND THE MADCAP ACTION OF THE THREE-RING CIRCUS. BUT DESPITE THE BILLIONS SPENT ON PRODUCTION AND STAGING, NOTHING CAN MATCH THE POWER OF MADONNA AND HER GIRLIE SHOW ENSEMBLE.

ALL OF THE MOST SOPHISTICATED AND POWERFUL TOOLS IN THE ARSENAL OF TEMPTATION WILL BE UNLEASHED IN ALL THEIR SPLENDID MAGNETISM.

NO
EMOTION
WILL
REMAIN
UN
TOUCH
ED

BUT FEAR NOT.

■ ENCHANTED MALES AND FEMALES ALIKE WILL BE MERCIFULLY RELEASED FROM ANY HYPNOTIC SPELLS THEY MAY HAVE FALLEN

UNDER AT THE END OF THE PERFORMANCE, OR A FULL REFUND WILL BE TENDERED.

YOU'LL BE
ASTONISHED
AND ASTOUNDED
YOU'LL BE
BEWITCHED
AND BEGUILED
YOU'LL BE
EDIFIED AND
CONFOUNDED
YOU'LL BE
THRILLED AND
FLABBERGASTED
SIMULTANEOUSLY

IT WILL
BRING
GOOSEBUMPS
TO YOUR
SKIN

A TEAR
TO YOUR
EYE

IT WILL BRING A LUMP TO YOUR **THROAT** AND POSSIBLY TO YOUR TROUSERS

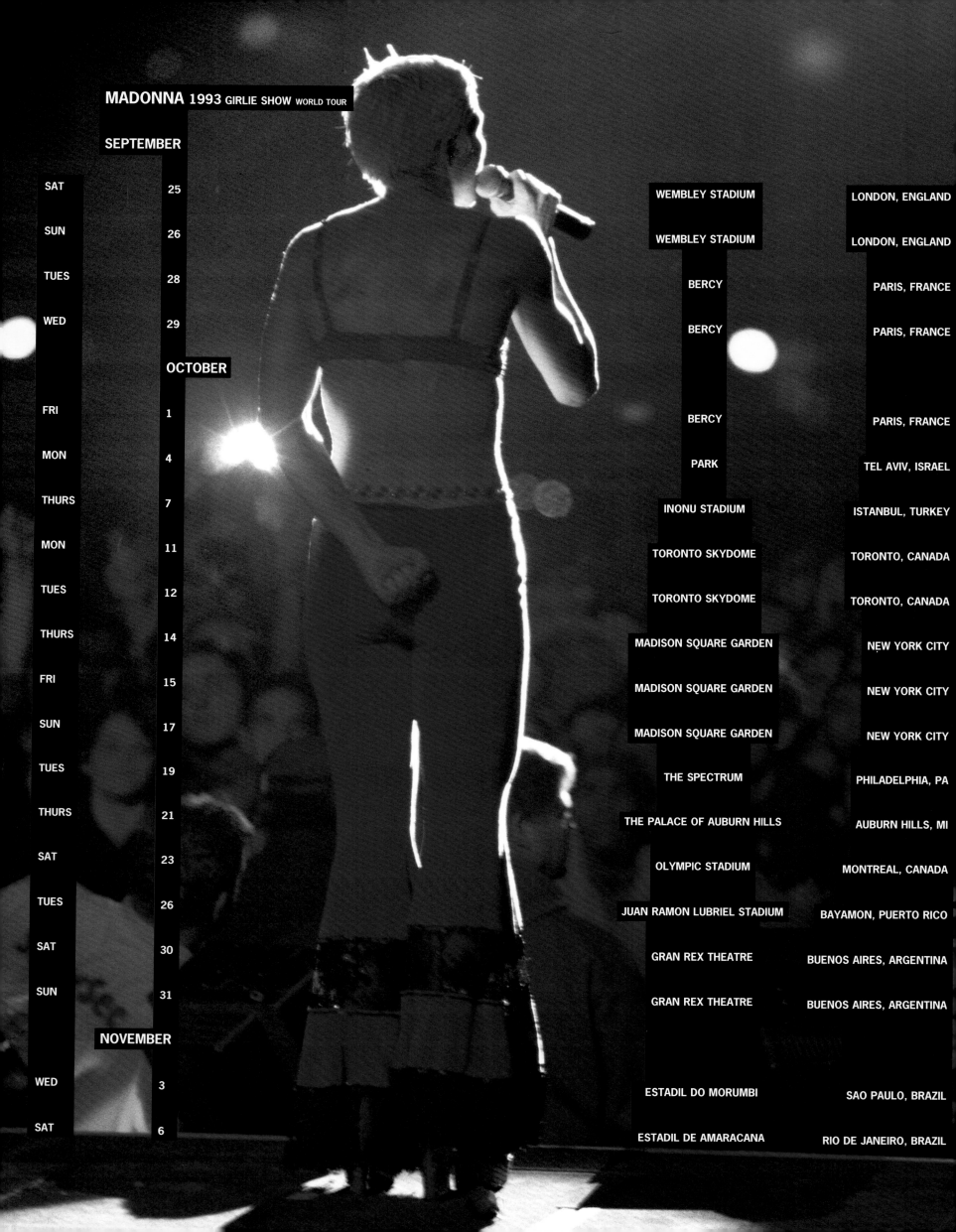

MADONNA 1993 GIRLIE SHOW WORLD TOUR

SEPTEMBER

SAT	25	WEMBLEY STADIUM	LONDON, ENGLAND
SUN	26	WEMBLEY STADIUM	LONDON, ENGLAND
TUES	28	BERCY	PARIS, FRANCE
WED	29	BERCY	PARIS, FRANCE

OCTOBER

FRI	1	BERCY	PARIS, FRANCE
MON	4	PARK	TEL AVIV, ISRAEL
THURS	7	INONU STADIUM	ISTANBUL, TURKEY
MON	11	TORONTO SKYDOME	TORONTO, CANADA
TUES	12	TORONTO SKYDOME	TORONTO, CANADA
THURS	14	MADISON SQUARE GARDEN	NEW YORK CITY
FRI	15	MADISON SQUARE GARDEN	NEW YORK CITY
SUN	17	MADISON SQUARE GARDEN	NEW YORK CITY
TUES	19	THE SPECTRUM	PHILADELPHIA, PA
THURS	21	THE PALACE OF AUBURN HILLS	AUBURN HILLS, MI
SAT	23	OLYMPIC STADIUM	MONTREAL, CANADA
TUES	26	JUAN RAMON LUBRIEL STADIUM	BAYAMON, PUERTO RICO
SAT	30	GRAN REX THEATRE	BUENOS AIRES, ARGENTINA
SUN	31	GRAN REX THEATRE	BUENOS AIRES, ARGENTINA

NOVEMBER

WED	3	ESTADIL DO MORUMBI	SAO PAULO, BRAZIL
SAT	6	ESTADIL DE AMARACANA	RIO DE JANEIRO, BRAZIL

WED	10	PALACIO DE LOS DEPO	MEXICO CITY
FRI	12	PALACIO DE LOS DEPO	MEXICO CITY
SAT	13	PALACIO DE LOS DEPO	MEXICO CITY
FRI	19	SYDNEY CRICKET GROUND	SYDNEY, AUSTRALIA
SAT	20	SYDNEY CRICKET GROUND	SYDNEY, AUSTRALIA
WED	24	BRISBANE ANZ STADIUM	BRISBANE, AUSTRALIA
FRI	26	MELBOURNE CRICKET GROUND	MELBOURNE, AUSTRALIA
SAT	27	MELBOURNE CRIGKET GROUND	MELBOURNE, AUSTRALIA
MON	29	MELBOURNE CRICKET GROUND	MELBOURNE, AUSTRALIA

DECEMBER

WED	1	ADELAIDE OVAL	ADELAIDE, AUSTRALIA
FRI	3	SYDNEY CRICKET GROUND	SYDNEY, AUSTRALIA
SAT	4	SYDNEY CRICKET GROUND	SYDNEY, AUSTRALIA
TUES	7	FUKUOKA DOME	FUKUOKA, JAPAN
WED	8	FUKUOKA DOME	FUKUOKA, JAPAN
THURS	9	FUKUOKA DOME	FUKUOKA, JAPAN
MON	13	TOKYO DOME	TOKYO, JAPAN
TUES	14	TOKYO DOME	TOKYO, JAPAN
THURS	16	TOKYO DOME	TOKYO, JAPAN
FRI	17	TOKYO DOME	TOKYO, JAPAN
SUN	19	TOKYO DOME	TOKYO, JAPAN

DIRECTOR AND PRODUCTION DESIGNER: CHRISTOPHER G. CICCONE
MUSICAL DIRECTOR: JAI WINDING
ENTIRE PRODUCTION STAGED BY: JEFFREY HORNADAY
CHOREOGRAPHED BY: ALEX MAGNO AND KEITH YOUNG
ADDITIONAL CHOREOGRAPHY: MICHELLE JOHNSTON AND NIKI HARIS
COSTUMES: DOLCE AND GABBANA
ADDITIONAL COSTUMES: ROB SADUSKI
VIDEO DIRECTOR: MARK "ALDO" MICELI

THE BAND:
KEYBOARDS: JAI WINDING, MICHAEL BEARDEN
GUITAR: PAUL PESCO
BASS: VICTOR BAILEY
DRUMS: OMAR HAKIM • PERCUSSION: LUIS CONTE
ADDITIONAL KEYBOARDS: MIKE McKNIGHT
BACKGROUND VOCALS: NIKI HARIS, DONNA DeLORY
DANCERS: UNGELA BROCKMAN, CHRISTOPHER CHILDERS, MICHAEL GREGORY, CARRIE ANN INABA,
JILL NICKLAUS, RUTH INCHAUSTEGUI, LUCA TOMMASSINI, CARLTON WILBORN

THIS IS A CALLAWAY BOUNDSOUND™ BOOK, PUBLISHED BY CALLAWAY EDITIONS, INC.

COPYRIGHT © 1994 BOY TOY, INC.

COMPACT DISC ℗ 1994 BOY TOY, INC.

PHOTOGRAPHS COPYRIGHT © 1994 BY BOY TOY, INC., NEAL PRESTON,
CHRISTOPHER G. CICCONE, AND BOY TOY, INC./HERB RITTS PHOTOGRAPHY, INC.

LIBRARY OF CONGRESS CATALOG CARD NUMBER 94-72271 ISBN 0-935112-22-7

THIS PUBLICATION IS AN ADAPTATION FROM THE GIRLIE SHOW TOUR PROGRAM, LICENSED BY WINTERLAND PRODUCTIONS.

COMPACT DISC PRODUCED BY JAI WINDING PRODUCTIONS, INC.

COMPACT DISC TRACK CREDITS:

IN THIS LIFE (M. CICCONE/S. PETTIBONE/T. SHIMKIN) WB MUSIC CORP./WEBO GIRL PUBLISHING, INC.
ADM. BY WB MUSIC CORP./SHEPSONGS ADM. BY MCA, INC. ASCAP. WHY'S IT SO HARD (M. CICCONE/S. PETTIBONE)
WB MUSIC CORP./WEBO GIRL PUBLISHING, INC. ADM. BY WB MUSIC CORP./SHEPSONGS ADM. BY MCA MUSIC PUBLISHING,
A DIVISION OF MCA, INC. ASCAP. LIKE A VIRGIN (B. STEINBERG/T. KELLY) SONY TUNES, INC. ASCAP.

TEXT BY GLENN O'BRIEN

TITLE PAGE ILLUSTRATION BY ROB SADUSKI

PHOTOGRAPHS BY

NEAL PRESTON, PAGES 7, 12, 15, 16-17, 24, 26-27, 30-31, 33, 36-37, 40-41, 42, 50-51, 53, 54, 60, AND BACK COVER;

CHRISTOPHER G. CICCONE, PAGES 8, 10-11, 20, 44, 49, 58-59, 62-63;

HERB RITTS, PAGES 4, 22, 25, 56, FRONT COVER AND CD ENVELOPE;

SERGE THOMANN, PAGES 28, 34-35, 39, 61;

MELODIE MCDANIEL, PAGES 2-3, 47;

SIUNG FAT TJIA, PAGE 18.

DESIGNED BY ROGER GORMAN AND RICK PATRICK OF REINER DESIGN CONSULTANTS, INC.

PRODUCED UNDER THE DIRECTION OF NICHOLAS CALLAWAY, EDITORIAL DIRECTOR.

COORDINATED AND EDITED BY ANDREA DANESE.

PRODUCTION COORDINATED BY TRUE SIMS WITH THE ASSISTANCE OF MAY BLOOMER AND MARION HECK.

SPECIAL THANKS TO THE FOLLOWING INDIVIDUALS FOR THEIR HELP IN CREATING THIS BOOK:

MADONNA'S PERSONAL ASSISTANT, CARESSE HENRY, PAUL SCHINDLER AND HIS ASSISTANTS BARBARA BENJAMIN AND ROBERTA WHITING,

DAVID TORAYA, MATT GREENBERG, FREDDY DEMANN AND HIS ASSISTANT RENEE SANDMAN, MO OSTIN, MICHAEL KRASSNER, YVONNE CHANG,

AND LIZ ROSENBERG AND HER ASSISTANT CHRISTINE SCHACHTER.

PRINTED IN JAPAN BY TOPPAN PRINTING CO., LTD. PRINTING SUPERVISION BY SHIZUO MATSUZAKA.

FIRST EDITION

10 9 8 7 6 5 4 3 2 1

THE OFFICIAL MADONNA FAN CLUB
MARCIA DEL VECCHIO/COORDINATOR
8491 SUNSET BOULEVARD #485
WEST HOLLYWOOD, CA 90069

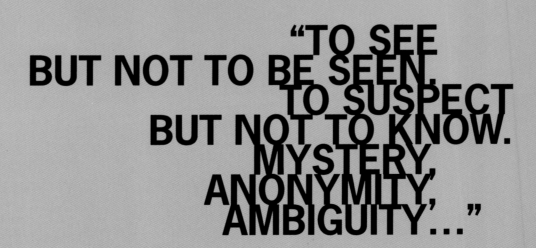

"TO SEE
BUT NOT TO BE SEEN.
TO SUSPECT
BUT NOT TO KNOW.
MYSTERY,
ANONYMITY,
AMBIGUITY'..."

GORE VIDAL

כפארק רי

ה · י · ו · נ

כרטיסים בכל המ

03-5279449 "הדרן", 03-5279797 "השרון" 2/5400551-03, חיפה:

17 , משרד הפקה: 02-2568